CONTENTS

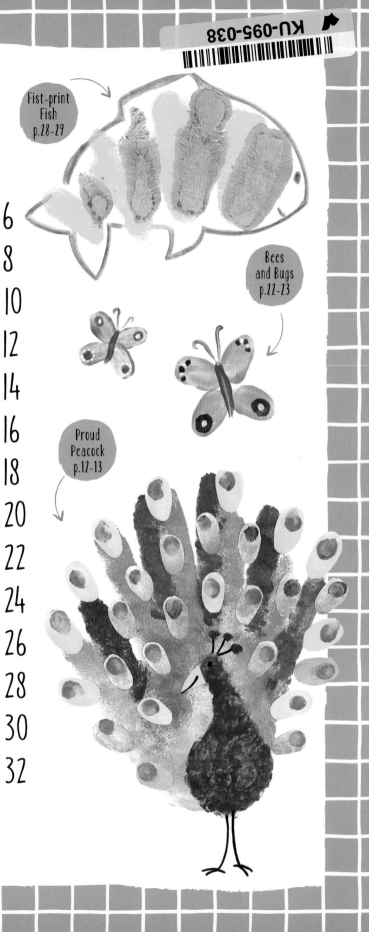

Fist-print Fish p.28-29

Bees and Bugs p.22-23

Proud Peacock p.12-13

LET'S MAKE ART!

LOOK AT THE SHAPES OF YOUR HANDS AND FEET — WHAT DO THEY SAY TO YOU? CAN YOU SEE A BIRD, A FISH, A DINOSAUR OR AN AEROPLANE? IF NOT, YOU SOON WILL AFTER READING THIS BOOK!

WHAT YOU NEED

Making a handprint, footprint or fingerprint is a brilliant way of starting a picture. All you need are a few basic art supplies, plus your very own fingers and toes! Look in the recycling for old envelopes, brown paper and cardboard that you can use as a background for your work. Scraps of wrapping paper, wallpaper or magazine pages are great for extra bits of decoration.

FOR THE PROJECTS IN THIS BOOK IT ALSO HELPS TO HAVE THE FOLLOWING MATERIALS:

- ✓ ready-mix paints
- ✓ newspaper
- ✓ paintbrushes
- ✓ a sponge
- ✓ coloured ink pads
- ✓ a pencil and rubber
- ✓ scissors
- ✓ glue
- ✓ plain white paper or card
- ✓ coloured paper or card, including black
- ✓ coloured pencils
- ✓ felt-tip pens
- ✓ wool or ribbon
- ✓ bubble wrap
- ✓ a hole punch

4

SUSIE BROOKS

LET'S MAKE ART

WITH

HANDS AND FEET

Published in paperback in Great Britain in 2019 by Wayland

Copyright © Hodder and Stoughton, 2016

All rights reserved.
ISBN: 978 1 5263 0042 3
10 9 8 7 6 5 4 3 2 1

Printed in Dubai

Wayland
An imprint of
Hachette Children's Group
Part of Hodder and Stoughton
Carmelite House
50 Victoria Embankment
London EC4Y 0DZ

An Hachette UK Company
www.hachette.co.uk
www.hachettechildrens.co.uk

Editor: Elizabeth Brent
Design: nicandlou
With special thanks to Bing Meddowes for the use of his hands and feet.

HANDY HINTS

Before you start, lay down plenty of newspaper to protect the surface you're working on.

Keep a bowl of water, a cloth and a towel nearby to clean your hands and feet as you work. Kitchen paper is useful for wiping, too.

It can take a few goes to make a perfect print. Try these tips:
- cover the underside of your hand or foot evenly with paint - a sponge is useful for doing this
- press your hand or foot firmly down on the paper and KEEP IT STILL to avoid smudging
- lift your hand or foot straight up again afterwards, holding down the paper with your other hand.

Sometimes painted paper wrinkles as it dries. Don't worry - you can flatten it later under a pile of books.

Always wait for your print to dry before painting or sticking on details.

When you see this LOGO, you might want to ask an adult to help.

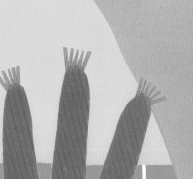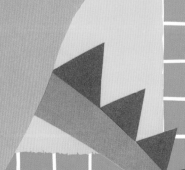

BLUE ZOO

YOU CAN MAKE A WHOLE ZOO OF FRIENDLY ANIMALS OUT OF YOUR HANDPRINTS — EVEN USING JUST ONE COLOUR!

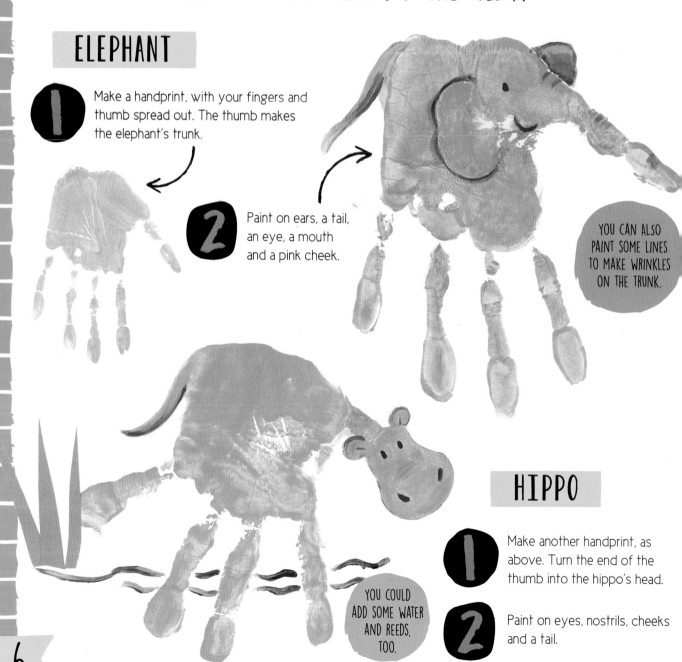

ELEPHANT

1 Make a handprint, with your fingers and thumb spread out. The thumb makes the elephant's trunk.

2 Paint on ears, a tail, an eye, a mouth and a pink cheek.

YOU CAN ALSO PAINT SOME LINES TO MAKE WRINKLES ON THE TRUNK.

HIPPO

1 Make another handprint, as above. Turn the end of the thumb into the hippo's head.

2 Paint on eyes, nostrils, cheeks and a tail.

YOU COULD ADD SOME WATER AND REEDS, TOO.

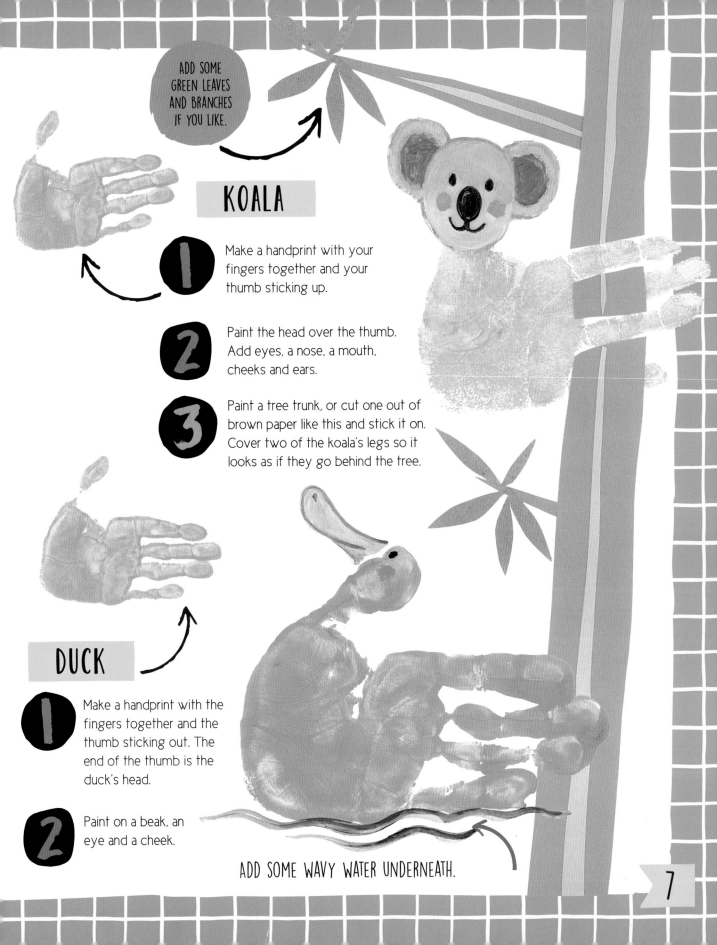

ADD SOME GREEN LEAVES AND BRANCHES IF YOU LIKE.

KOALA

1 Make a handprint with your fingers together and your thumb sticking up.

2 Paint the head over the thumb. Add eyes, a nose, a mouth, cheeks and ears.

3 Paint a tree trunk, or cut one out of brown paper like this and stick it on. Cover two of the koala's legs so it looks as if they go behind the tree.

DUCK

1 Make a handprint with the fingers together and the thumb sticking out. The end of the thumb is the duck's head.

2 Paint on a beak, an eye and a cheek.

ADD SOME WAVY WATER UNDERNEATH.

PLAYFUL PENGUINS

USE THESE FUN FOOTPRINT PENGUINS TO MAKE A PICTURE OR EVEN A GREETINGS CARD.

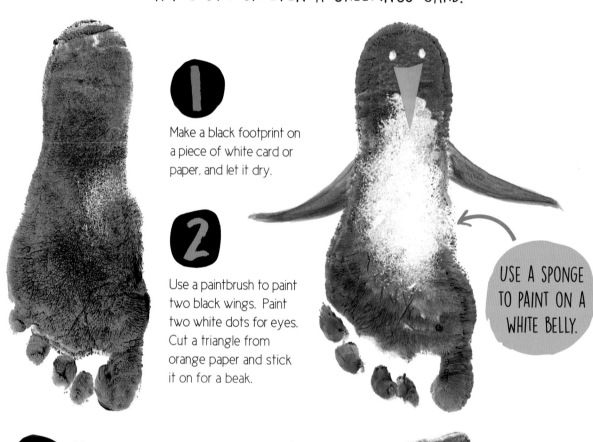

1 Make a black footprint on a piece of white card or paper, and let it dry.

2 Use a paintbrush to paint two black wings. Paint two white dots for eyes. Cut a triangle from orange paper and stick it on for a beak.

USE A SPONGE TO PAINT ON A WHITE BELLY.

3 You can make a handprint into a sledging penguin. Keep your fingers and thumb together when you print.

PAINT ON A HEAD AND ADD A BEAK AND EYES AS ABOVE.

THIS SLOPE IS CUT FROM BLUE PAPER, WITH WHITE PAINT DABBED ON IT USING A SPONGE.

DRAW A SMILEY LINE ON THE BEAK.

USE BOTH FEET TO MAKE A PAIR OF SKIPPING PENGUINS!

Here's something else you can try. Draw around your hand on white paper. Cut it out and stick it on to blue card. Now turn each finger into a penguin on an ice block.

PAINT THE BODIES AND STICK ON ORANGE BEAKS AND FEET.

DOTTY DELIGHTS

YOU CAN MAKE LOTS OF PRETTY PATTERNS WITH FINGERPRINT DOTS! FOR GIFT TAGS OR DECORATIONS, DO THIS ON SMALL PIECES OF CARD. USE A CLOTH OR KITCHEN PAPER TO WIPE YOUR FINGER WHEN YOU CHANGE COLOUR.

PROJECT 1 Start with the middle dot, then surround it with circles of dots in a different colour. Add as many circles as you like.

PROJECT 2 For this pattern, start with the middle dot, then add more dots to make a square shape, like this one.

TO MAKE A DOT, DIP THE TIP OF YOUR FINGER IN PAINT AND DAB IT LIGHTLY ON TO PAPER.

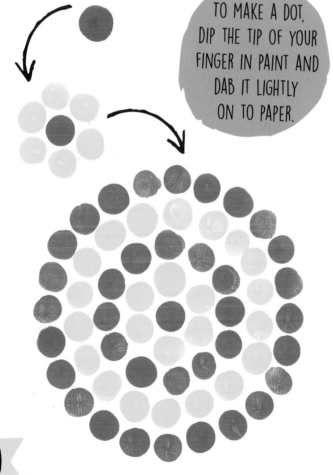

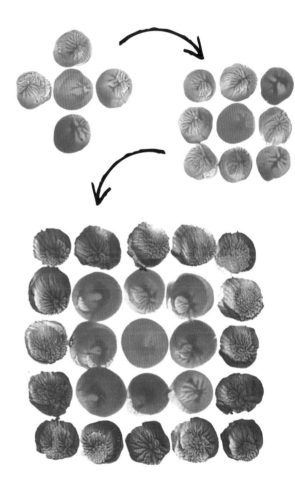

10

Start with a line of dots, then turn it into a cross. Fill in L-shapes in the corners until you have a complete square.

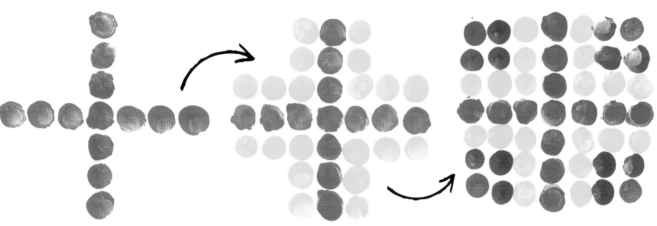

TO MAKE A GIFT TAG, CUT OUT YOUR DOTTY PATTERN. MAKE A HOLE NEAR ONE EDGE USING A HOLE PUNCH. THREAD THROUGH SOME WOOL OR RIBBON AND KNOT THE ENDS.

tip

You could stick your pattern on to coloured card.

PROUD PEACOCK

TURN A HAND STENCIL INTO A BEAUTIFUL BIRD PICTURE!

1 Draw around your hand on thin cardboard. Cut it out, keeping the outside part whole. This outside part is your stencil.

2 Lay the stencil on to white card or paper. Use a sponge to dab light-blue paint over the hand shape.

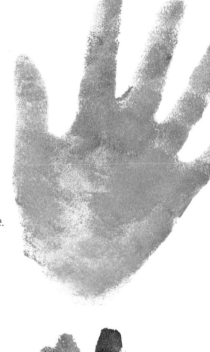

3 When the paint is dry, lay the stencil back on the paper so the fingers of the stencil are between the fingers of the blue hand. Dab dark blue paint into the stencil fingers.

DRAW ON THE EYE, HEAD FEATHERS AND LEGS.

4 Dip your finger in the dark blue paint and use it to paint the peacock's body.

CUT OUT YELLOW PA TRIANGLE MAKE A BE

5 For the tail tips, make lots of green and yellow thumbprints on a piece of white paper. Add fingerprint dots in a different colour on top.

CUT OUT THE TAIL TIPS AND GLUE THEM TO YOUR PEACOCK.

YOU COULD ALSO TRY A SIDEWAYS PEACOCK, LIKE THIS ONE!

13

FACES IN A CROWD

YOU CAN HAVE FUN WITH THUMBPRINT FACES! COLOURED INK PADS AND FELT TIPS WORK WELL FOR THIS.

1 Make a row of thumbprints and try drawing on faces like these:

HAPPY

PUZZLED

SURPRISED

SAD

2 Practise drawing different hairstyles and expressions.

A ROUND MOUTH FOR A YAWN.

3 You can draw a neck and shoulders, or add a body using more thumbprints.

THERE'S A CAT UP A TREE.

THESE PEOPLE ARE LOOKING OVER A FINGERPRINT WALL.

4
Make a collection of faces in a crowd scene.

ARE SOME PEOPLE IN A HURRY? WHERE ARE THEY GOING? THINK UP A STORY TO GO WITH YOUR SCENE!

FAST FEET

TURN YOUR FOOTPRINTS INTO SPEEDY VEHICLES! YOU CAN USE THE TEMPLATES ON P.30 TO HELP YOU.

RACING CAR

1 Make a coloured footprint and let it dry.

2 Cut out shapes for the wheels, spoiler and driver's helmet.

3 On a scrap of white paper, make a thumbprint and draw on a face. Cut this out and stick it on to the helmet.

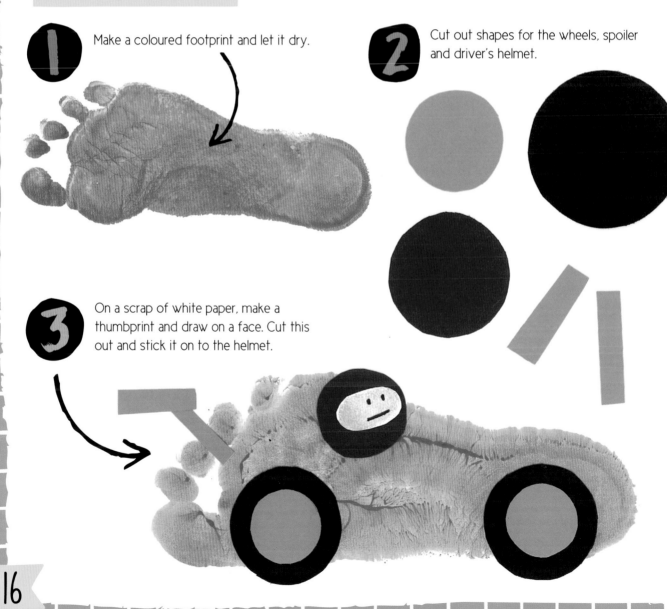

AEROPLANE

1 Make a coloured footprint and leave it to dry.

2 Stick on coloured paper shapes for the wings and tail.

3 Add some rows of windows – you could draw, paint or fingerprint them on.

THESE WINDOWS WERE MADE FROM A WHITE STRIP OF PAPER WITH BLACK SQUARES DRAWN ON.

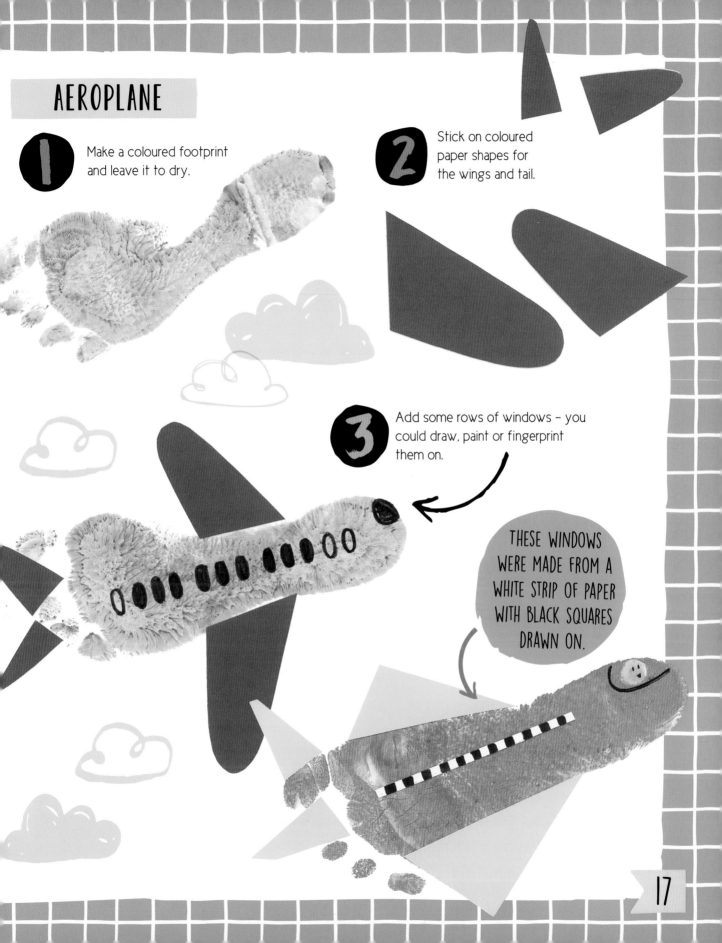

HANDY DINOSAURS

MAKE YOUR HANDS INTO DIFFERENT SHAPES TO CREATE THESE BRIGHT BEASTIES!

tip

For each dinosaur, draw around your hand on coloured paper, as shown in the outline. Cut it out and glue it on to a paper or card background, then stick on the dinosaur features.

PROJECT 1

Draw and cut out a hand shape with fingers and thumb spread out. Cut a separate tail shape and glue it on.

THIS LITTLE WHITE PAPER CIRCLE CAME OUT OF A HOLE PUNCH! DRAW ON A BLACK DOT.

ADD TRIANGLES FOR THE SPIKE AND NOSE.

PROJECT 2

Curl your hand into a fist but leave your thumb pointing out. Draw around your hand, and cut it out.

CUT OUT SHAPES FOR THE LEGS, TAIL AND SPIKES.

DRAW ON A SMILEY FACE.

18

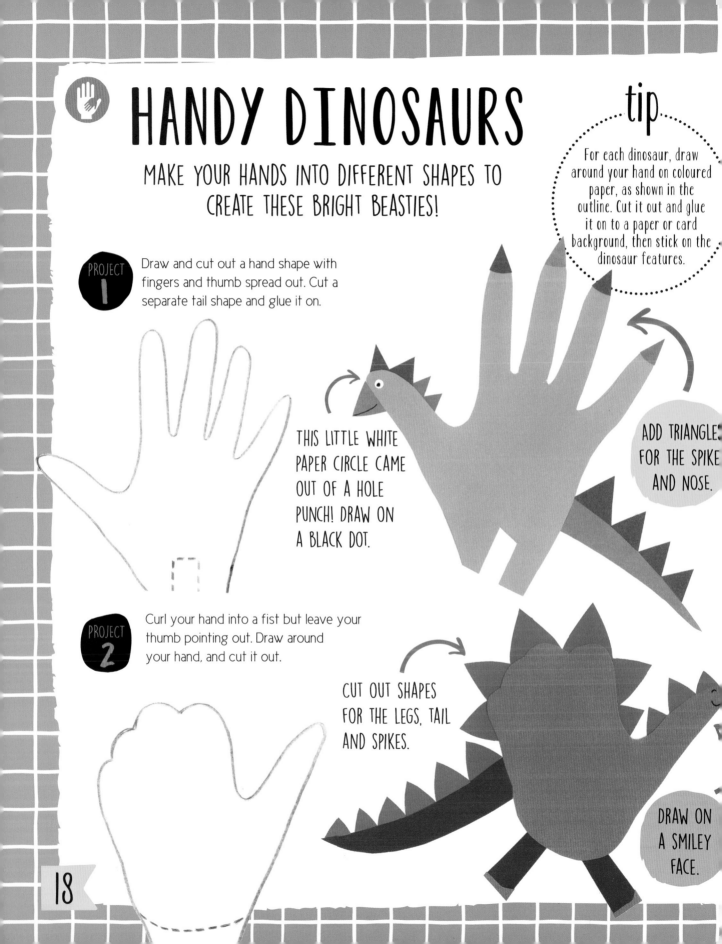

PROJECT 3

Rest your hand on its side with the fingers together and the thumb below them. When you've drawn around and cut out the shape, stick on paper circles and triangles for the eye, cheek and teeth.

FINGERPRINT SOME DOTS ON THE DINOSAUR.

PROJECT 4

Draw and cut out a flat hand shape, then turn it upside down and trim it straight across the top. Cut out shapes for the neck frill, horns and tail.

PROJECT 5

To make a plant like this, draw around a flat hand on corrugated paper and cut off the finger section. Snip some pink paper to make the flowers, and stick them to each fingertip.

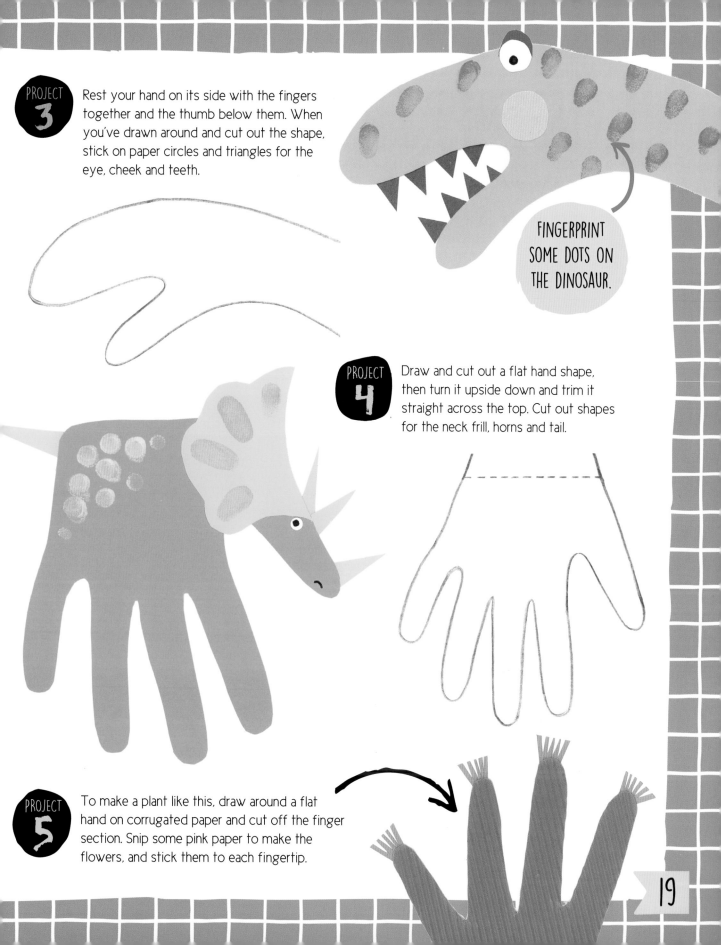

FINGERPRINT SWEET SHOP

YOU CAN MAKE A WHOLE SWEET SHOP'S WORTH OF TASTY TREATS, USING JUST COLOURED INK PADS, PENCILS AND PAPER.

 Start by drawing the outline of a jar.

 Press your fingertip on to a brightly coloured ink pad and print lots of dots inside the jar. Do one colour, then wipe your finger clean and print another colour.

THESE SWEETS ARE MADE FROM THUMBPRINTS. DRAW ON THE WRAPPERS AFTERWARDS.

 For a lolly, make two thumbprints in a heart shape, or fingerprint some dots in a circle. Draw on the sticks and an outline if you like.

 You can turn lots of dots into a cupcake or a sundae! There are some templates on p.31 to help with the bases, if you need.

5 Why not make a whole range of sweet treats, and cut them out to stick in your own sweet shop!

Use coloured paper for the background, and glue on long, thin strips in a different colour for shelves.

TRY MAKING DIFFERENT LIDS FOR YOUR JARS. YOU CAN DRAW THEM OR CUT THEM OUT FROM SCRAP PAPER.

TRY CUTTING OUT A CUPCAKE CASE FROM OLD WRAPPING PAPER, LIKE THIS.

BEES AND BUGS

TURN YOUR FINGER— AND THUMBPRINTS INTO
A COLLECTION OF CUTE CREEPY CRAWLIES!

THIS BUTTERFLY IS MADE FROM FOUR THUMBPRINTS WITH A PAINTED BODY AND MARKINGS

BUMBLE BEE

1 Make a yellow thumbprint. Add two white wings using the tip of your index finger.

2 When the paint has dried, draw on the markings with a black pen.

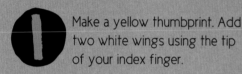

SPIDER

1 Paint white dots on a dark thumbprint, then draw black dots for the eyes.

2 Add eight legs and a web or dangly thread!

LADYBIRD

1 Make a red thumbprint and let it dry.

2 Draw on the ladybird's dots and six legs.

TRY ADDING SOME CURLY ANTENNAE.

22

THUMBPRINT A SWARM OF BEES BUZZING TO AND FROM THE HONEYCOMB!

TO PRINT A HONEYCOMB LIKE THIS, CUT A SHAPE OUT OF BUBBLE WRAP. COVER THE BUBBLY SIDE WITH PAINT, THEN PRESS IT ON TO PAPER.

FLOWERS

1 Make a green thumbprint, then paint a stalk with a paintbrush. Let the paint dry before printing a clump of white dots with your fingertip.

HAUNTED HANDS

MAKE THESE SPOOKY GHOSTS WITH WHITE PAINT ON BLACK CARD, AND PIN THEM UP TO HAUNT YOUR HOUSE FOR HALLOWEEN.

Make a white handprint and let it dry. Use black paint or a marker to add a scary face.

A WHITE FOOTPRINT CAN BE SPOOKY TOO.

FOR THIS SKELETON, MAKE A FIST WITH YOUR THUMB TUCKED IN, AND DIP YOUR BENT FINGERS INTO THE PAINT. MAKE A PRINT, THEN PAINT ON A SKULL AND SOME ARMS.

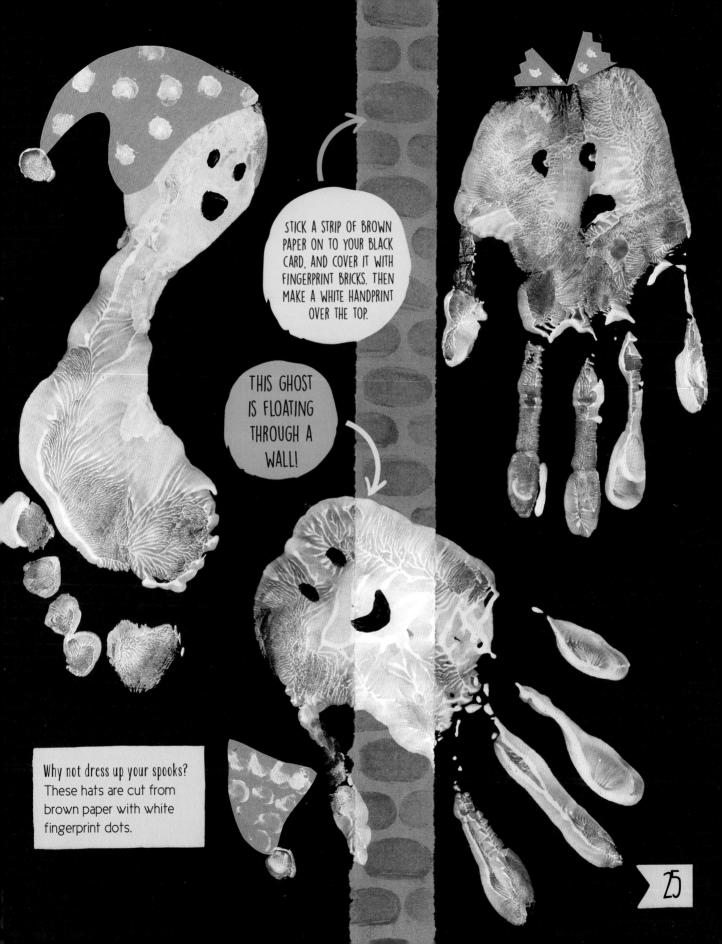

STICK A STRIP OF BROWN PAPER ON TO YOUR BLACK CARD, AND COVER IT WITH FINGERPRINT BRICKS. THEN MAKE A WHITE HANDPRINT OVER THE TOP.

THIS GHOST IS FLOATING THROUGH A WALL!

Why not dress up your spooks? These hats are cut from brown paper with white fingerprint dots.

THUMBPRINT CIRCUS

COLOURED INK PADS ARE USEFUL FOR MAKING THESE LIVELY CIRCUS CHARACTERS.

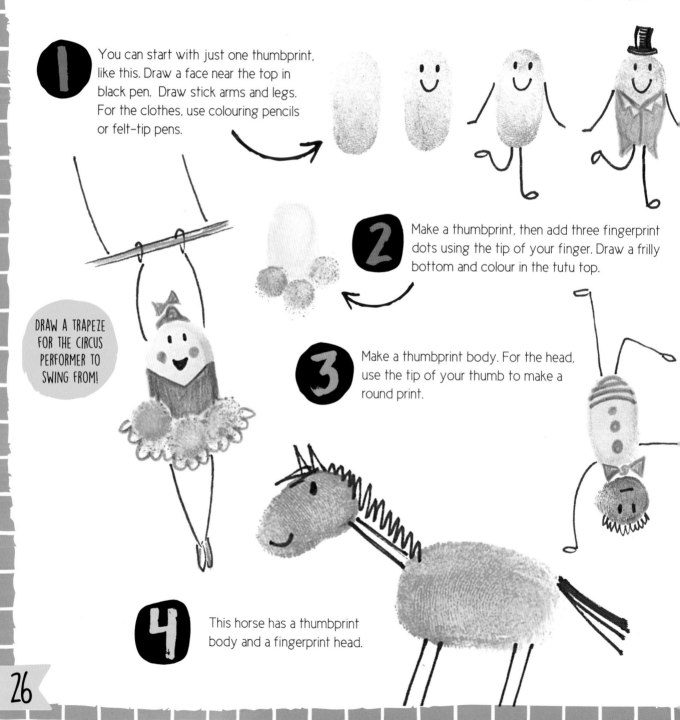

1 You can start with just one thumbprint, like this. Draw a face near the top in black pen. Draw stick arms and legs. For the clothes, use colouring pencils or felt-tip pens.

2 Make a thumbprint, then add three fingerprint dots using the tip of your finger. Draw a frilly bottom and colour in the tutu top.

3 Make a thumbprint body. For the head, use the tip of your thumb to make a round print.

DRAW A TRAPEZE FOR THE CIRCUS PERFORMER TO SWING FROM!

4 This horse has a thumbprint body and a fingerprint head.

FINGERTIP PRINT SOME BALLOONS!

YOU COULD ADD SOME FACES IN THE CROWD.

5 Try making a whole circus scene! Print the performers first, then paint or colour in a yellow circus ring and some big-top stripes around them.

FIST-PRINT FISH

CLENCH YOUR FIST TO MAKE A WHOLE SHOAL OF THESE FANTASTIC FISH.

1 Hold your fist with your palm facing downwards and your thumb tucked in, and dip your bent fingers into some paint. Press your fist on to white paper.

2 When the paint is dry, draw the outline of a fish around it. There are templates on p.31 if you need.

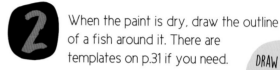

DRAW ON AN EYE AND A MOUTH.

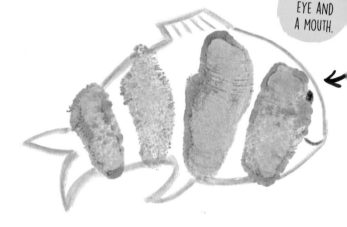

3 For this fish, add another colour! Print a yellow fist and let it dry. Then clean your hand, dip it in pink paint and print a fist over the top, in the gaps.

4 For this fish, print one fist above another.

MAKE THE TAIL AND BOTTOM FIN FROM THUMBPRINTS.

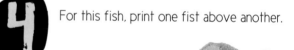

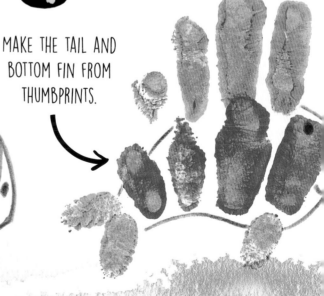

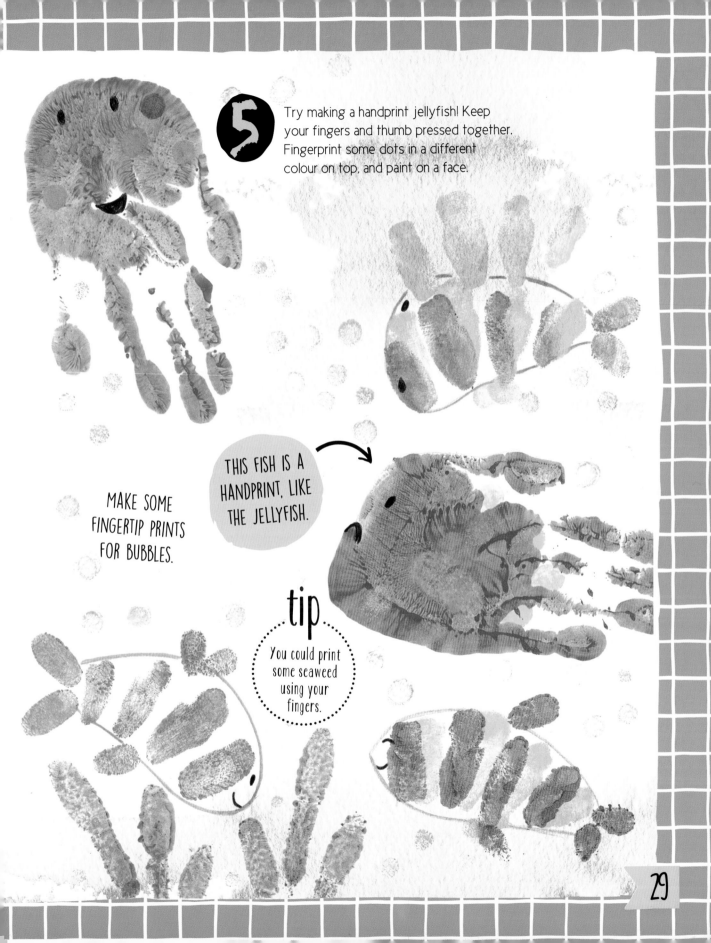

5 Try making a handprint jellyfish! Keep your fingers and thumb pressed together. Fingerprint some dots in a different colour on top, and paint on a face.

THIS FISH IS A HANDPRINT, LIKE THE JELLYFISH.

MAKE SOME FINGERTIP PRINTS FOR BUBBLES.

tip
You could print some seaweed using your fingers.

TEMPLATES

FAST FEET
P.16—17

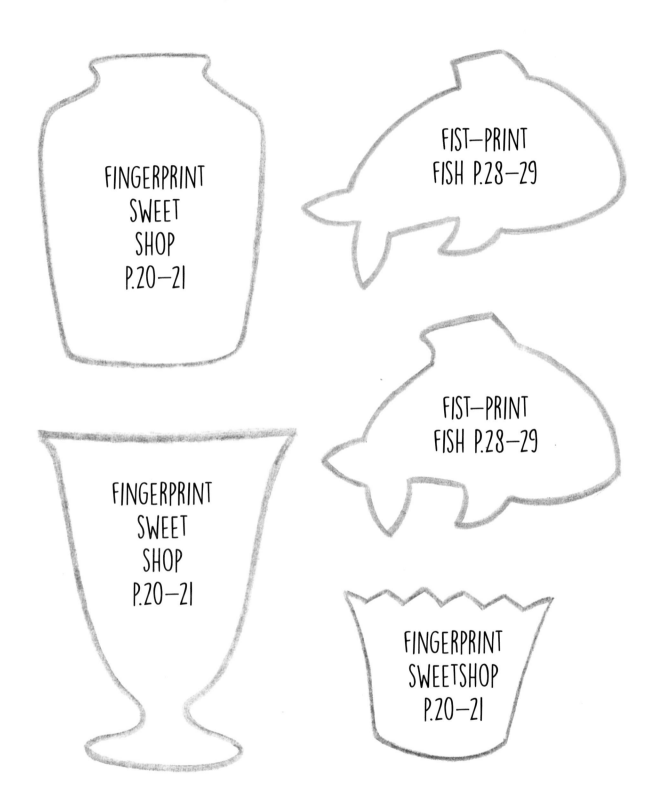

FINGERPRINT
SWEET
SHOP
P.20–21

FIST–PRINT
FISH P.28–29

FIST–PRINT
FISH P.28–29

FINGERPRINT
SWEET
SHOP
P.20–21

FINGERPRINT
SWEETSHOP
P.20–21

GLOSSARY

COLLAGE art made by sticking bits of paper, fabric or other materials on to a surface

CORRUGATED ridged, like the inside layer of some cardboard

INDEX FINGER the finger next to your thumb

OUTLINE a line showing the shape of an object

PRINT an image made by pressing a painted or inked object on to paper, card or another surface. The printed image comes out in reverse.

STENCIL a thin piece of cardboard (or other material) with a shape cut out of it. A design can be made by placing the stencil on paper and applying paint or ink through the hole.

TEMPLATE a shape used as a guideline to draw or cut around